CW00385626

Prayers Given to

To Change the World and Change

The World by Changing Ourselves

The Holy Rosary, The Rosary of Sorrows the Chaplet of Mercy and other Devotions

By Richard Dole

© 2022 All Rights Reserved

† Imprimatur Daniel Cardinal Dinardo

Archdiocese of Galveston-Houston

October 9, 2019

All Scripture texts in this work are taken from the New American Bible, revised edition © 2010, Confraternity of Christian Doctrine, Washington, D.C. and are used by permission of the copyright owner. All Rights Reserved. No part of the New American Bible may be reproduced in any form without permission in writing from the copyright owner.

Previously Published Under the Title "Prayers Given to Us to Change the World by Changing Ourelves"

Cover Art by Raíza Pantoja

raizapantoja@gmail.com

One may have good intentions and understand what it means to live a chaste and spiritually healthy life, but still repeatedly fall short. One reason for this may be that an individual underestimates the reality of what it takes to shoulder their cross daily and follow Jesus. Pride says, "I know what to do, it is easy..." whereas fear and shame convince one that it is too hard, so why try. It is worse, of course, if all these impediments are operating at the same time. if one lacks the power necessary to simultaneously do battle with myself, the world and the prince of this world--what is one to do? The power heaven through the Lord Jesus is the answer and his life, cross and resurrection testify to this.

The resurrection and ascension the were witnessed by those who stated them as fact. All of the Christian martyrs gave their lives as further witness of these truths. Charles Colson was convicted in the Watergate scandal in the early 1970's and had a conversion experience in prison. He noted that the twelve most powerful men in America could not maintain a lie for three weeks, whereas the apostles all told the same truth for 40 years or more while suffering and dying because of it. By their own testimony they were first empowered by the spirit of God at Pentecost when the holy spirit was poured out among them. They ran forth from their hiding place and out into the street boldly proclaiming the truth of God and Our risen Lord Jesus. The same God who did that will accomplish the same in us if we allow Him. There is no question that God, who formed all that there is in creation out of nothing, also has the power to aid us in overcoming the world, temptation and the dark powers.

How does one tap into the power to overcome what our limited strength and will cannot do? The lives of the saints are full of stories of virtue triumphing over sin, death, the world and satan. We have at our disposal the same spiritual weapons that the saints have used for millennia to empower themselves. The greatest gift one can have in striving to follow Christ is a relationship with Him. This is accomplished with a mode of meditation that allows Our Lord to speak and a manner of prayer that enables us to converse with Him. Like all children we tend to be better at talking than listening. This may be one of the reasons why some of us are slower to learn than others. It is in an intimate relationship with God that one can act in faith, find themselves redirected and empowered by the One Person who loves us more than anyone on earth. The fact is that Person is the source of all love coming to us through others. Therefore, it is a love more tender than that of a mother for a newborn child. It is a love that would rather face death than think of heaven without us.

The western tradition is rich in ways with which to relate to our Maker. It has puzzled me that so many take up eastern traditions while being entirely ignorant of the rich history meditation and mysticism in the Judeo-Christian tradition. What follows are some powerful, meaningful and simple ways to speak and listen to God. He can bring out the goodness He sees in us even when we are at our worst. Hopefully these tools of our faith will enrich your relationship with the One Who Loves us, making your interior world and the world we share a better place.

The 15 Promises of the Mother of God Made to

St. Dominic and Bl. Alan de la Roche regarding the rosary:

To all those who shall recite my Rosary devoutly, I promise my special protection and very great graces.

Those who shall persevere in the recitation of my Rosary shall receive some signal grace.

The Rosary shall be a very powerful armor against hell; it will destroy vice, deliver from sin, and dispel heresy.

The Rosary will make virtue and good works flourish and will obtain for souls the most abundant...divine mercies; it will substitute in hearts love of God for love of the world and will lift them to the desire of heavenly and eternal things. How many souls shall sanctify themselves by this means!

Those that trust themselves to me through the Rosary shall not perish.

Those who shall recite my Rosary devoutly, meditating on its mysteries, shall not be overwhelmed by misfortune. The sinner shall be converted; the just shall grow in grace and become worthy of eternal life.

Those truly devoted to my Rosary shall not die without the Sacraments of the Church.

Those who recite my Rosary shall find during their life and at their death the light of God, the fullness of His graces, and shall share in the merits of the blessed.

I shall deliver very promptly from purgatory the souls devoted to my Rosary.

The true children of my Rosary shall enjoy great glory in heaven.

What you ask through my Rosary, you shall obtain.

Those that propagate my Rosary shall be aided by me in all their necessities.

I have obtained from my Son that all the members of the Rosary Confraternity shall have for their brethren the saints of heaven during their life and at the hour of death.

Those who recite my Rosary faithfully are all my beloved children, the brothers and sisters of Jesus Christ.

Devotion to my Rosary is a great sign of predestination.

Prayers of the Rosary:

Kiss the Crucifix.

The Apostle's Creed-said on the crucifix:

I believe in God, the Father Almighty, Creator of heaven and earth; and in Jesus Christ, HIs only Son, our Lord. He was conceived by the power of the Holy Spirit, born of the Virgin Mary. Suffered under Pontius Pilate, was crucified, died and was buried. He descended into hell. On the third day He rose again from the dead; He ascended into heaven, and is seated at the right hand of, the Father Almighty; from thence He shall come to judge the living and the dead. I believe in the Holy Spirit, the Holy Catholic Church, the communion of saints, the forgiveness of sins, the resurrection of the body and the life everlasting. Amen.

The Our Father-said on the large beads at the beginning of each decade:

Our Father, who art in heaven, hallowed be Thy name; Thy kingdom come; Thy will be done on earth as it is in heaven. Give us this day our daily bread; and forgive us our trespasses as we forgive those who trespass against us; and lead us not into temptation but deliver us from evil. Amen.

The Hail Mary-said on the ten beads after the Our Father:

Hail Mary, full of grace, the Lord Is with thee, blessed art thou amongst women and blessed is the fruit of thy womb, Jesus. Holy Mary Mother of God pray for us sinners now and at the hour of our death. Amen.

The Glory be-said on the chains at the end of each decade:

Glory be to the Father, and to the Son, and to the Holy Spirit. As it was in the beginning, is now, and ever shall be, world without end. Amen.

After the Glory be and said on the chains, the Fatima Prayer:

"Oh, my Jesus, forgive us our sins. Save us from the fires of hell. Lead all souls to Heaven, especially those in most need of Thy Mercy."

Hail Holy Queen said at the conclusion of the rosary:

Hail Holy Queen, mother of mercy, our life our sweetness our hope. To you do we send up our sighs mourning and weeping in this valley of tears. Turn then, most gracious advocate, your eyes of mercy toward us and after this our exile and show unto us the most blessed fruit of your womb, Jesus. O clement, O loving, O sweet Virgin Mary. Pray for us O holy mother of God that we may be made worthy of the promises of Christ. Amen.

Optional closing prayer:

God whose only begotten Son has purchased for us the rewards of eternal life. Grant, we beseech you, that in meditating upon theses mysteries of the holy rosary of the Blessed Virgin Mary, we may imitate what they contain and obtain what they promise through Christ Our Lord. Amen.

May the divine assistance remain always with us and the souls of the faithful departed rest in peace. Amen.

Prayer to St. Joseph After the Rosary:

This prayer was written by Pope Leo XIII in 1898--the same pope who was inspired to write the prayer to St. Michael the Archangel. He assigned indulgences to it and asked that it be said after the rosary, especially in October which is the month dedicated to the rosary. It may also be said after other Marian devotions (i).

To you, O blessed Joseph,
do we come in our tribulation,
and having implored the help of your most holy Spouse,
we confidently invoke your patronage also.

Through that charity which bound you
to the Immaculate Virgin Mother of God
and through the paternal love
with which you embraced the Child Jesus,
we humbly beg you graciously to regard the inheritance
which Jesus Christ has purchased by his Blood,
and with your power and strength to aid us in our necessities.

O most watchful guardian of the Holy Family,
defend the chosen children of Jesus Christ;

O most loving father, ward off from us
every contagion of error and corrupting influence;
O our most mighty protector, be kind to us
and from heaven assist us in our struggle
with the power of darkness.

As once you rescued the Child Jesus from deadly peril,
so now protect God's Holy Church
from the snares of the enemy and from all adversity;
shield, too, each one of us by your constant protection,
so that, supported by your example and your aid,
we may be able to live piously, to die in holiness,
and to obtain eternal happiness in heaven. Amen.

Spiritual Communion:

Lord, I am not worthy that Thou should enter under my roof, but only say the word and my soul shall be healed.

My Jesus, I believe that you are present in the Blessed Sacrament. I love you above all things and I desire you in my soul. Since I cannot now receive you in the Blessed Sacrament, come at least spiritually into my heart. As though you were already there, I embrace you and unite myself to you; permit not that I should ever be separated from you. Amen.

The Mysteries of Joy

To be said on Mondays and Saturdays

The Annunciation of Our Lord:

Fruit of the mystery-humility

St John Paul II: "...the whole of the universe is in some way touched by the divine favor with which the Father looks upon Mary and makes her the Mother of his Son. The whole of humanity, in turn, is embraced by the fiat with which she readily agrees to the will of God," *Rosarium Virgins Mariae paragraph 20. Our Father.*

And coming to her, he said, "Hail, favored one! The Lord Is with you (Lk 1:28)!" *Hail Mary.*

Then the angel said to her, "Do not be afraid, Mary, for you have found favor with God (Lk 1:30)."

"Behold, you will conceive in your womb and bear a son, and you shall name him Jesus (Lk 1:31)."

"He will be great and will be called Son of the Most High, and the Lord God will give him the throne of David his father (Lk 1:32)."

"...he will rule over the house of Jacob forever, and of his kingdom there will be no end (Lk 1:33)."

But Mary said to the angel, "How can this be, since I have no relations with a man (Lk 1:34)?"

"The Holy Spirit will come upon you, and the power of the Most High will overshadow you. Therefore, the child to be born will be called holy, the Son of God (Lk 1:35)."

Mary said, "Behold, I am the handmaid of the Lord. May it be done to me according to your word." Then the angel departed from her (Lk 1:38).

Therefore, the Lord himself will give you a sign the young woman, pregnant and about to bear a son, shall name him Emmanuel (Is 7:14).

The angel of the Lord appeared to him in a dream and said, "Joseph, son of David, do not be afraid to take Mary your wife into your home. For it is through the Holy Spirit that this child has been conceived in her (Mt 1:20)." *Glory be, O my Jesus.*

The Visitation of Mary to Elizabeth:

Fruit of the mystery-service to others and love of neighbor

St John Paul II: "Exultation is the keynote of the encounter with Elizabeth, where the sound of Mary's voice and the presence of Christ in her womb cause John to "leap for joy cf. Lk 1:44)," *Rosarium Virgins Mariae* paragraph 20. *Our Father.*

When Elizabeth heard Mary's greeting, the infant leaped in her womb, (Lk 1:41). *Hail Mary.*

Elizabeth filled with the Holy Spirit, "Most blessed are you among women, and blessed is the fruit of your womb (Lk 1:42)."

"And how does this happen to me that the mother of my Lord should come to me (Lk 1:43)?"

"Blessed are you who believed that what was spoken to you by the Lord would be fulfilled (Lk 1:45)."

"My soul proclaims the greatness of the Lord; my spirit rejoices in God my savior (Lk 1:46-47)."

"For he has looked upon his handmaid's lowliness; behold, from now on will all ages call me blessed (Lk 1:48)."

"The Mighty One has done great things for me, and holy is his name (Lk 1:49)."

"He has shown might with his arm, dispersed the arrogant of mind and heart (Lk 1:51)."

"He has thrown down the rulers from their thrones but lifted up the lowly (Lk 1:52)."

"The hungry he has filled with good things; the rich he has sent away empty (Lk 1:53)." *Glory be, O my Jesus.*

The Birth of Our Lord:

Fruit of the mystery-detachment from the world

St John Paul II; "O Mary, bright dawn of the new world, Mother of the living, to you do we entrust the cause of life," *General Audience: The Solemnity of the Annunciation of the Lord 1995. Our Father.*

In the beginning was the Word, and the Word was with God, and the Word was God (Jn 1:1). *Hail Mary*

Yours Is princely power from the day of your birth. In holy splendor before the daystar, like dew I begot you (Ps 110:3).

You formed my inmost being; you knit me in my mother's womb (Ps 139:13).

But you, Bethlehem-Ephrathah least among the clans of Judah, from you shall come forth for me one who Is to be ruler in Israel; Whose origin Is from of old, from ancient times (Mi 5:1).

...she gave birth to her firstborn son. She wrapped him in swaddling clothes and laid him in a manger, because there was no room for them in the inn (Lk 2:7).

"I proclaim to you good news of great joy that will be for all the people. For today in the city of David a savior has been born for you who Is Messiah and Lord (Lk 2:10-11)."

And suddenly there was a multitude of the heavenly host with the angel, praising God and saying: "Glory to God in the highest and on earth peace to those on whom his favor rests (Lk 2-13-14)."

When they saw this, they made known the message that had been told them about this child (Lk. 2:17).

And this will be a sign for you: you will find an infant wrapped in swaddling clothes and lying in a manger (Lk 2:12)."

And Mary kept all these things, reflecting on them in her heart (Lk 2:19). *Glory be, O my Jesus.*

The Presentation of Our Lord at the Temple:

Fruit of the mystery-obedience

St. John Paul II: "It is to focus on the realism of the mystery of the Incarnation and on the obscure foreshadowing of the mystery of the saving Passion," *Rosarium Virgins Mariae paragraph 20. Our Father.*

The fear of the LORD Is pure, enduring forever. The statutes of the LORD are true, all of them just (Ps 19:10). *Hail Mary.*

When the days were completed for their purification according to the Law of Moses, they took him up to Jerusalem to present him to the Lord (Lk 2:22).

Just as it is written in the law of the Lord, "Every male that opens the womb shall be consecrated to the Lord (Lk 2:23)."

And to offer the sacrifice of "a pair of turtledoves or two young pigeons," in accordance with the dictate in the law of the Lord (Lk 2:24).

"Now, Master, you may let your servant go in peace, according to your word (Lk 2:29)."

"For my eyes have seen your salvation, which you prepared in sight of all the peoples (Lk 2:30-31)."

"A light for Revelation to the Gentiles, and glory for your people Israel (Lk 2:32)."

Simeon blessed them and said to Mary his mother, "Behold, this child is destined for the fall and rise of many in Israel, and to be a sign that will be contradicted (Lk 2:34)."

"(And you yourself a sword will pierce). So that the thoughts of many hearts may be revealed (Lk 2:35)."

The child's father and mother were amazed at what was said about him; (Lk 2:33). *Glory be, O my Jesus.*

The Finding of Our Lord in the Temple:

Fruit of the mystery-piety and seeking God

St John Paul II: "Here he appears in his divine wisdom as he listens and raises questions, already in effect one who "teaches". The Revelation of his mystery as the Son wholly dedicated to his Father's affairs proclaims the radical nature of the Gospel..." *Rosarium Virginis Mariae paragraph 20. Our Father.*

Each year his parents went to Jerusalem for the feast of Passover (Lk 2:41). *Hail Mary.*

After they had completed its days, as they were returning, the boy Jesus remained behind in Jerusalem, but his parents did not know it (Lk 2:43).

Thinking that he was in the caravan, they journeyed for a day and looked for him among their relatives and acquaintances (Lk 2:44).

But not finding him, they returned to Jerusalem to look for him (Lk 2:45).

After three days they found him in the temple, sitting in the midst of the teachers, listening to them and asking them questions (Lk 2:46).

When his parents saw him, they were astonished, and his mother said to him, "Son, why have you done this to us? Your father and I have been looking for you with great anxiety (Lk 2:48)."

And he said to them, "Why were you looking for me? Did you not know that I must be in my Father's house (Lk 2:49)?"

The LORD begot me, the beginning of his works, the forerunner of his deeds of long ago (Prv 8:22);

The fear of the Lord Is wisdom; and avoiding evil is understanding (Job 28:28).

Keep my commands and live, and my teaching as the apple of your eye (Prv 7:2). *Glory be, O my Jesus.*

The Mysteries of Light *said on Thursday*

The Baptism of Our Lord:

Fruit of the mystery-being open to the Holy Spirit

St John Paul II: "Here, as Christ descends into the waters, the innocent one who became 'sin' for our sake (cf. 2Cor 5:21), the heavens open wide and the voice of the Father declares him the beloved Son (cf. Mt. 3:17), while the Spirit descends on him to invest him with the mission which he is to carry out," *Rosarium Virginis Mariae paragraph 21. Our Father.*

I will proclaim the decree of the LORD, he said to me, "You are my son; today I have begotten you (Ps. 2:7)." *Hail Mary.*

During the high priesthood of Annas and Caiaphas, the word of God came to John the son of Zechariah in the desert (Lk 3:2).

He went throughout [the] whole region of the Jordan..., proclaiming a baptism of repentance for the forgiveness of sins (Lk. 3:3).

"I am baptizing you with water, but one mightier than I Is coming. I am not worthy to loosen the thongs of his sandals. He will baptize you with the Holy Spirit and fire (Lk 3:16)."

"His winnowing fan is in his hand. He will clear his threshing floor and gather his wheat into his barn, but the chaff he will burn with unquenchable fire (Mt 3:12)."

"I need to be baptized by you, and yet you are coming to me (Mt 3:14)?"

After Jesus was baptized, he came up from the water and behold, the heavens were opened [for him], and he saw the Spirit of God descending like a dove [and] coming upon him (Mt. 3:16).

And a voice came from the heavens, saying, "This is my beloved Son, with whom I am well pleased (Mt 3:17)."

"The one who has the bride is the bridegroom; the best man, who stands and listens to him, rejoices greatly at the bridegroom's voice. So, this joy of mine has been made complete (Jn 3:29)."

"He must increase; I must decrease (Jn. 3:30)." *Glory be, O my Jesus.*

The Wedding at Cana:

Fruit of the mystery-going to Our Lord through our blessed mother

St John Paul II: "When Christ changes water into wine and opens the hearts of the disciples to faith, thanks to the intervention of Mary, the first among believers," *Rosarium Virginis Mariae* paragraph 21. *Our Father.*

On the third day there was a wedding in Cana in Galilee, and the mother of Jesus was there (Jn 2:1). *Hail Mary.*

When the wine ran short, the mother of Jesus said to him, "They have no wine (Jn 2:3)."

Jesus said to her, "Woman, how does your concern affect me? My hour has not yet come (Jn 2:4)."

HIs mother said to the servers, "Do whatever he tells you (Jn. 2:5)."

Jesus told them, "Fill the jars with water." So, they filled them to the brim (Jn 2:7)."

Then he told them, "Draw some out now and take it to the headwaiter." So, they took it (Jn 2:8).

The headwaiter called the bridegroom and said to him, "Everyone serves good wine first, and then when people have drunk freely, an inferior one; but you have kept the good wine until now (Jn 2:9-10)."

Jesus did this as the beginning of his signs in Cana in Galilee and so Revealed his glory, and his disciples began to believe in him (Jn 2:11).

As a bridegroom rejoices in his bride so shall your God rejoice in you (Is 62:5).

I also saw the holy city, a new Jerusalem, coming down out of heaven from God, prepared as a bride adorned for her husband (Rv. 21:2). *Glory be, O my Jesus.*

Our Lord Proclaims His Kingdom:

Fruit of the mystery-repentance and trust in God

St John Paul II: "Jesus proclaims the coming of the Kingdom of God, calls to conversion (Mk. 1:15) and forgives the sins of all who draw near to him in humble trust (Mk. 2:3-13; Lk. 7:47- 48): the inauguration of that ministry of mercy which he continues to exercise until the end of the world," *Rosarium Virginis Mariae paragraph 2. Our Father.*

"The Spirit of the Lord Is upon me, because he has anointed me to bring glad tidings to the poor (Lk 4:18)." *Hail Mary.*

"He has sent me to proclaim liberty to captives and recovery of sight to the blind, to let the oppressed go free (Lk 4:19)."

"To proclaim a year acceptable to the Lord." He said to them, "Today this scripture passage is fulfilled in your hearing. (Lk 4:19, 4:21)."

And he said, "Amen, I say to you, no prophet is accepted in his own native place (Lk 4:24)."

"This is the time of fulfillment. The kingdom of God Is at hand. Repent, and believe in the gospel (Mk 1:15)."

They were filled with great awe and said to one another, "Who then is this whom even wind and sea obey (Mk 4:19)?"

At sunset, all who had people sick with various diseases brought them to him. He laid his hands on each of them and cured them (Lk 4:40).

And demons also came out from many, shouting, "You are the Son of God." But he rebuked them and did not allow them to speak because they knew that he was the Messiah (Lk 4:41).

"And so I say to you, you are Peter, and upon this rock I will build my church, and the gates of the netherworld shall not Prevail against it (Mt 16:18)."

There are also many other things that Jesus did, but if these were to be described individually, I do not think the whole world would contain the books that would be written (Jn 21:25). *Glory be, O my Jesus.*

The Transfiguration:

Fruit of the mystery-a desire for holiness

St John Paul II: "Christ's transfiguration...can be seen as *an icon of Christian contemplation*. To look upon the face of Christ, to recognize its mystery amid the daily events and the sufferings of his human life..." *Rosarium Virginis Mariae* paragraph 9. *Our Father*.

Jesus took Peter, James, and John his brother, and led them up a high mountain by themselves (Mt. 17:10). *Hail Mary*.

And he was transfigured before them; his face shone like the sun and his clothes became white as light (Mt 17:2).

And behold, Moses and Elijah appeared to them, conversing with him (Mt 17:3).

Then Peter said to Jesus in reply, "Lord, it is good that we are here. If you wish, I will make three tents here, one for you, one for Moses, and one for Elijah (Mt 17:4)."

While he was still speaking, behold, a bright cloud cast a shadow over them, then from the cloud came a voice that said, "This Is my beloved Son, with whom I am well pleased; listen to him (Mt 17:5)."

When the disciples heard this, they fell prostrate and were very much afraid (Mt 17:6).

But Jesus came and touched them, saying, "Rise, and do not be afraid (Mt 17:7)."

And when the disciples raised their eyes, they saw no one else but Jesus alone (Mt 17:8).

Thrones were set up and the Ancient of Days took his throne. His clothing was white as snow, the hair on his head like pure wool (Dn 7:9).

HIs body was like chrysolite, his face shone like lightning, his eyes were like fiery torches, his arms and feet looked like burnished bronze (Dn 10:6). *Glory be, O my Jesus.*

The institution of the Eucharist:

Fruit of the mystery-appreciation of God

St John Paul II: "I am with you always, to the end of the age" (Mt. 22.20). This promise of Christ never ceases to resound in the Church as the fertile secret of her life and the well spring of her hope...It Is a celebration of the living presence of the Risen Lord in the midst of His own people," *Dies Domini paragraph 31. Our Father.*

But this is the covenant I will make with the house of Israel after those days—oracle of the LORD. I will place my law within them and write it upon their hearts (Jer 31:31). *Hail Mary.*

"For the bread of God Is that which comes down from heaven and gives life to the world (Jn 6:33)."

Jesus said to them, "I am the bread of life; whoever comes to me will never hunger, and whoever believes in me will never thirst (Jn 6:35)."

But they said to him, "Five loaves and two fish are all we have here (Mt 14:17)."

Then, taking the five loaves and the two fish and looking up to heaven, he said the blessing, broke the loaves, and gave them to his disciples, (Mk 6:41).

Those who ate were about five thousand men, not counting women and children (Mt 14:21).

Whoever drinks the water I shall give will never thirst; the water I shall give will become in him a spring of water welling up to eternal life (Jn 4:14)."

Then he took the bread, said the blessing, broke it, and gave it to them, saying, "This Is my body, which will be given for you; do this in memory of me (Mt 22:19)."

Then he took a cup, gave thanks, and gave it to them, saying, "Drink from it, all of you for this is my blood of the covenant, which will be shed on behalf of many for the forgiveness of sins (Mt 2:27-28)."

" And behold, I am with you always, until the end of the age (Mt 28:20)." *Glory be, O my Jesus.*

The Mysteries of Sorrow

To be said on Tuesdays and Fridays

The Agony of Our Lord in the Garden:

Fruit of the mystery-contrition and surrender to God's Will

St John Paul II: "Christ experiences a moment of great anguish before the will of the Father, against which the weakness of the flesh would be tempted to rebel. "Not my will but yours be done" (Lk. 22:42). This "Yes" of Christ Reverses the "No" of our first parents in the Garden of Eden," *Rosarium Virginis Mariae paragraph 22. Our Father.*

And while they were eating, he said, "Amen, I say to you, one of you will betray me (Mt 26:21)" *Hail Mary.*

Deeply distressed at this, they began to say to him one after another, "Surely it is not I, Lord (Mt 26:22)?"

Jesus said to him, "Amen, I say to you, this very night before the cock crows, you will deny me three times (Mt 26:34)."

Then he said to them, "My soul is sorrowful even to death. Remain here and keep watch with me (Mt 26:38)."

My soul thirsts for God, the living God. When can I enter and see the face of God (Ps 42:3)?

When he returned to his disciples, he found them asleep. He said to Peter, "So you could not keep watch with me for one hour (Mt 26:40)?"

"Watch and pray that you may not undergo the test. The spirit is willing, but the flesh is weak (Mt 26:41)."

"My Father, if it is not possible that this cup pass without my drinking it, your will be done (Mt 26: 42)."

Deep calls to deep in the roar of your torrents, and all your waves and breakers sweep over me (Ps 4:28).

Jesus said to him, "Judas, are you betraying the Son of Man with a kiss (Lk 22:48)?" *Glory be, O my Jesus.*

The Scourging of Our Lord:

Fruit of the mystery-mortification

St John Paul II: "...shows how humanity, subjected to sin, in the descendants of the first Adam, in Jesus Christ became perfectly subjected to God and united to him, and at the same time full of compassion towards men," Dominium et Veificantem paragraph 41. *Our Father.*

He bore the punishment that makes us whole, by his wounds we were healed (Is 53:5). *Hail Mary.*

Though he had done no wrong, nor was deceit found in his mouth.

So, Pilate said to him, "Then you are a king?" Jesus answered, "You say I am a king (Jn 18:37)."

"For this I was born and for this I came into the world, to testify to the truth. Everyone who belongs to the truth listens to my voice. (Jn 18:37)."

Pilate said to him, "What Is truth (Jn 18:38)?"

But all together they shouted out, "Away with this man! Release Barabbas to us (Lk 23:18)."

Pilate addressed them a third time, "What evil has this man done? I found him guilty of no capital crime. Therefore, I shall have him flogged and then release him (Lk 23:22)."

Pilate said to them, "Then what shall I do with Jesus called Messiah?" They all said, "Let him be crucified (Lk 27:22)."

But he said, "Why? What evil has he done?" They only shouted the louder, "Let him be crucified (Mt 27:23)."

He took water and washed his hands in the sight of the crowd, saying, "I am innocent of this man's blood. Look to it yourselves (Mt 27:24)." *Glory be, O my Jesus.*

Our Lord Is Crowned with Thorns:

Fruit of the mystery-humility and moral courage

St John Paul II: "God in Christ crucified acquires through the Holy Spirit its full human expression. Thus, there is a paradoxical mystery of love: in Christ there suffers a God who has been rejected by his own creature..." *Dominium et Vivificantem paragraph 41. Our Father.*

Like a lamb led to slaughter or a sheep silent before shearers, he did not open his mouth (Is 53:7). *Hail Mary.*

They stripped off his clothes and threw a scarlet military cloak about him (Mt 27:28).

Weaving a crown out of thorns, they placed it on his head, and a reed in his right hand. And kneeling before him, they mocked him, saying, "Hail, King of the Jews (Mt 27:29)!"

They spat upon him and took the reed and kept striking him on the head (Mt 27:30).

I gave my back to those who beat me, my cheeks to those who tore out my beard (Is 50:6);

My face I did not hide from insults and spitting (Is 50:6).

The Lord GOD Is my help, therefore I am not disgraced (Is 50:7).

I have set my face like flint, knowing that I shall not be put to shame (Is 50:7).

A bruised reed he will not break, and a dimly burning wick he will not quench (Is 42:3).

And when they had mocked him, they stripped him of the cloak, dressed him in his own clothes, and led him off to crucify him (Mt 27:31). *Glory be, O my Jesus.*

Our Lord Carries the Cross:

Fruit of the mystery-patience

St John Paul II: "*Following Christ* is not an outward imitation, since it touches man at the very depths of his being. Being a follower of Christ means *becoming conformed to him* who became a servant even to giving himself on the Cross," *Veritatis Splendor paragraph 21. Our Father.*

Then he said to all, "If anyone wishes to come after me, he must deny himself and take up his cross daily and follow me, (Lk 9:23)." *Hail Mary.*

"Whoever does not carry his own cross and come after me cannot be my disciple (Lk 14:27)."

"For whoever wishes to save his life will lose it, but whoever loses his life for my sake will save it (Lk 9:24)."

Yet it was our pain that he bore, our sufferings he endured (Is 53:4).

My servant, the just one, shall justify the many; their iniquity he shall bear (Is 53:11).

As they were going out, they met a Cyrenian named Simon; this man they pressed into service to carry his cross (Mt 27:32).

"No disciple is above his teacher, no slave above his master (Mt 10:24)."

"Take my yoke upon you and learn from me, for I am meek and humble of heart (Mt 11:29)."

"...you will find rest for yourselves. For my yoke is easy, and my burden light (Mt 11:29-30)."

"But the one who perseveres to the end will be saved (Mt. 24:13). *Glory be, O my Jesus.*

The Crucifixion of Our Lord:

Fruit of the mystery- perseverance and self-sacrifice

St John Paul II: "This abject suffering reveals not only the love of God but also the meaning of man himself. *Ecce homo*: the meaning, origin and fulfillment of man Is to be found in Christ, the God who humbles himself out of love "even unto death, death on a cross (Phil 2:8)," *Rosarium Virginis Mariae paragraph 22. Our Father.*

When they came to the place called the Skull, they crucified him and the criminals there, one on his right, the other on his left (Lk 23:33). *Hail Mary.*

But he was pierced for our sins, crushed for our iniquity (Is 53:5).

Then Jesus said, "Father, forgive them, they know not what they do." They divided his garments by casting lots (Lk 23:34).

The people stood by and watched; the rulers, meanwhile, sneered at him and said, "He saved others, let him save himself if he is the chosen one, the Messiah of God (Lk 23:35)."

"Aha! You who would destroy the temple and rebuild it in three days, save yourself by coming down from the cross (Mk 15:29-30)."

We had all gone astray like sheep, all following our own way; But the LORD laid upon him the guilt of us all (Is 53:6).

"Amen, I say to you, today you will be with me in Paradise. (Lk 23:43)."

And at three o'clock Jesus cried out in a loud voice, *"Eloi, Eloi, lema sabachthani?"* which is translated, "My God, my God, why have you forsaken me (Mk 15:34)?"

When Jesus had taken the wine, he said, "It Is finished." And bowing his head, he handed over the spirit (Jn 19:30).

The veil of the sanctuary was torn in two from top to bottom (Mk 15:38). *Glory be, O my Jesus.*

The Mysteries of Glory

The Resurrection:

Fruit of the mystery-faith

To be said on Wednesdays and Sundays

St John Paul II: "In the name of the Resurrection of Christ the Church proclaims life, which manifested itself beyond the limits of death, the life which is stronger than death. At the same time, she proclaims him who gives this life: The Spirit, the Giver of Life; she proclaims him and cooperates with him in giving life…" *Cominum et Vivicantem paragraph 58. Our Father.*

"They have taken the Lord from the tomb, and we don't know where they put him (Jn 20:2)." *Hail Mary.*

When Simon Peter arrived after him, he went into the tomb and saw the burial cloths there (Jn 20:6).

They said to them, "Why do you seek the living one among the dead (Lk 24:5)?"

And it happened that, while he was with them at table, he took bread, said the blessing, broke it, and gave it to them. With that their eyes were opened, and they recognized him, but he vanished from their sight (Lk 23:30-31).

"Look at my hands and my feet, that it is I myself. Touch me and see, because a ghost does not have flesh and bones as you can see, I have (Lk 24:39)."

He said to them, "These are my words that I spoke to you while I was still with you, that everything written about me in the law of Moses and in the prophets and Psalms must be fulfilled (Lk 24:44)."

And he said to them, "Thus it is written that the Messiah would suffer and rise from the dead on the third day (Lk 24:46)."

Jesus said to him, "Have you come to believe because you have seen me? Blessed are those who have not seen and have believed (Jn 20:29)."

He said to him the third time, "Simon, son of John, do you love me?" Peter was distressed that he had said to him a third time, "Do you love me (Jn 21:17?"

"Lord, you know everything; you know that I love you." [Jesus] said to him, "Feed my sheep (Jn 21:17)." *Glory be, O my Jesus.*

The Ascension:

Fruit of the mystery-hope

St John Paul II: "...we must keep alive the certainty that his ascension to heaven was not a departure, but only the transformation of a presence that does not fail. Christ is among us today; he is with us. 'I am with you always, until the end of the world (Mt. 28:20)'. Only here comes our strength, but also our consistency and our joy," *Homily for the Feast of the Ascension 1982 paragraph 2. Our Father.*

Then he led them [out] as far as Bethany, raised his hands, and blessed them (Lk 24:50). *Hail Mary.*

When they had gathered together, they asked him, "Lord, are you at this time going to restore the kingdom to Israel (Acts 1:6)?"

Then Jesus approached and said to them, "All power in heaven and on earth has been given to me (Mt 28:18)."

"It is not for you to know the times or seasons that the Father has established by his own authority (Acts 1:7)."

"But you will receive power when the Holy Spirit comes upon you, and you will be my witnesses in Jerusalem, throughout Judea and Samaria, and to the ends of the earth (Acts 1:8)."

"I will give you the keys to the kingdom of heaven. whatever you bind on earth shall be bound in heaven; and whatever you loose on earth shall be loosed in heaven (Mt 16:19)."

"Go, therefore, and make disciples of all nations, baptizing them in the name of the Father, and of the Son, and of the Holy Spirit (Mt 28:19)."

"Teaching them to observe all that I have commanded you. And behold, I am with you always, until the end of the age (Mt 28:20)."

As he blessed them, he parted from them and was taken up to heaven (Lk 24:51).

The LORD says to my lord: "Sit at my right hand, while I make your enemies your footstool (Ps 110:10)." *Glory be, O my Jesus.*

The Descent of the Holy Spirit:

Fruit of the mystery-wisdom and the love of God

St John Paul II: "Jesus during the discourse in the Upper Room foretells the coming of the Holy Spirit at the price of" his own departure, and promises 'I will send him to you," in the very same context he adds: 'And when he comes, he will convince the world concerning sin and righteousness and judgment'" (Jn 16:8), *Dominium et Vivificatem paragraph 29. Our Father*

When the time for Pentecost was fulfilled, they were all in one place together (Acts 2:1). *Hail Mary*

And suddenly there came from the sky a noise like a strong driving wind, and it filled the entire house in which they were (Acts 2:2).

Then there appeared to them tongues as of fire, which parted and came to rest on each one of them (Acts 2:3).

And they were all filled with the Holy Spirit and began to speak in different tongues, as the Spirit enabled them to proclaim (Acts 2:4).

Both Jews and converts to Judaism, Cretans and Arabs, yet we hear them speaking in our own tongues of the mighty acts of God (Acts 2:11)."

It shall come to pass I will pour out my spirit upon all flesh. Your sons and daughters will prophesy, your old men will dream dreams, your young men will see visions (Jl 3:1).

Before the day of the LORD arrives, that great and terrible day. Then everyone who calls upon the name of the LORD will escape harm (Jl 3:4-5).

I will pour out my spirit upon your offspring; my blessing upon your descendants (Is 44:3).

Those who accepted his message were baptized, and about three thousand persons were added that day (Acts 2:41).

Send forth your spirit, they are created; and you renew the face of the earth (Ps 104:30). *Glory be, O my Jesus.*

The Assumption of Our Blessed Mother to Heaven:

Fruit of the mystery-devotion to our blessed mother

St John Paul II: "Even now, amid the joyful songs of the heavenly Jerusalem, the reasons for her thanksgiving and praise remain unchanged. They inspire her maternal concern for the pilgrim Church, in which she continues to relate her personal account of the Gospel," *Rosarium Virginis Mariae* paragraph 11. *Our Father.*

In embroidered apparel she is led to the king (Ps 45:15). *Hail Mary.*

"You are the glory of Jerusalem! You are the great pride of Israel (Jdt 15:9)!"

"I am a flower of Sharon, a lily of the valleys (Sng 2:1)."

"Arise, my friend, my beautiful one, and come (Sng 2:10)!"

"Let me hear your voice, for your voice is sweet, and your face is lovely, (Sng 2:14)."

"You are beautiful in every way, my friend; there is no flaw in you (Sng 4:7)!"

"One alone is my dove, my perfect one, (Sng 6:9)."

"Deep waters cannot quench love, nor rivers sweep it away (Sng 8:7)."

"Swiftly, my lover, be like a gazelle or a young stag (Sng 8:14)."

"Who is this coming up from the desert, like columns of smoke perfumed with myrrh and frankincense, with all kinds of exotic powders (Sng 3:6)?" *Glory be, O my Jesus.*

The Coronation of Our Blessed Mother Queen of Heaven and Earth:

Fruit of the mystery-eternal happiness

St John Paul II: "Mary shares our human condition, but in complete openness to the grace of God. Not having known sin, she is able to have compassion for every kind of weakness. She understands sinful man and loves with a mother's love," *Veritatis Splendor paragraph 120. Our Father.*

"I will put enmity between you and the woman, and between your offspring and hers (Gn 3:15)" *Hail Mary.*

"They will strike at your head, while you strike at their heel (Gn 3:15)."

Then God's temple in heaven was opened, and the ark of his covenant could be seen in the temple (Rv 11:19).

A great sign appeared in the sky, a woman clothed with the sun, with the moon under her feet, and on her head a crown of twelve stars (Rv 12:1).

With an iron rod. Her child was caught up to God and his throne (Rv 12:5).

Then war broke out in heaven; Michael and his angels battled against the dragon. The dragon and its angels fought back (Rv 12:7).

But they did not prevail and there was no longer any place for them in heaven (Rv 12:8).

The huge dragon, the ancient serpent, who Is called the Devil and Satan, who deceived the whole world, was thrown down to earth, and its angels were thrown down with it (Rv 12:9).

Those who love me I also love, and those who seek me find me (Prv 8:17).

For whoever finds me finds life and wins favor from the LORD; (Prv 8:35). *Glory Be, O my Jesus, Hail Holy Queen.*

PROMISES FOR DEVOTION
TO OUR LADY'S SORROWS:

St. Alphonsus Liguori, in his book *The Glories of Mary* mentioned a revelation in which St. John the Evangelist saw both Our Lord and His Blessed Mother after her assumption into Heaven. He heard Mary ask Jesus for some special grace to all those who are devoted to her sorrows (ii). Christ promised the four following special graces:

That those before death who invoked the divine Mother in the name of her sorrows should obtain true repentance of all their sins.

That He would protect all who have this devotion in their tribulations, and that He would protect them especially at the hour of their death.

That He would impress upon their minds the remembrance of His Passion, and that they should have their reward for this in heaven.

That He would commit such devout clients to the hands of Mary, with the power to disposed of them in whatever manner she might please, and to obtain for them all the graces she might desire.

For her part, Our Blessed Mother revealed to St. Bridget of Sweden that she grants the following seven graces to the souls who honor her daily by saying seven Hail Marys while meditating on her tears and dolores (sorrows):

"I will grant peace to their families."

"They will be enlightened about the divine Mysteries."

35

"I will console them in their pains, and I will accompany them in their work."

"I will give them as much as they ask for as long as it does not oppose the adorable will of my divine Son or the sanctification of their souls."

"I will defend them in their spiritual battles with the infernal enemy and I will protect them at every instant of their lives."

"I will visibly help them at the moment of their death—they will see the face of their mother."

"I have obtained this grace from my divine Son, that those who propagate this devotion to my tears and dolores will be taken directly from this earthly life to eternal happiness, since all their sins will be forgiven, and my Son will be their eternal consolation and joy."

The Rosary of Our Lady of Sorrows:

The rosary Our Lady of Sorrows was first used in the city of Florence Italy by a group of devout merchants that were interested in a life of penance. Around the year 1240 they withdrew from the world and eventually formed into the Servite Order who devoted their prayer to Our Lady of Sorrow with this rosary. The seven sorrows of Mary are taken from scripture and trace the life of Our Lady from the presentation to Our Lord being laid in the tomb. In our own times Our Blessed Mother has come to us and urged that we employ this devotion with sincerity and a will to repent and return to God.

On July 2, 2001, the Holy See released the declaration approving the apparitions of Our Lady at Kibeho Rwanda. The apparitions began in 1981 at a boarding school for girls and encouraged repentance, prayer from the heart and sincere devotion. On

May 15, 1982 Our Lady related that *"No one gets to heaven without suffering...The Son of Mary is never separated from suffering."* Civil war erupted in Rwanda in 1990 and one million people were slaughtered in a genocidal frenzy that was predicted by Our Lady in the 1980's. In 1982 Our Lady came to plead with people and related that if her instructions were followed the death seen by the visionaries could be avoided. On May 31, 1982, Our Lady said to Marie Claire: *"What I ask of you is repentance. If you recite this chaplet, while meditating on it, you will then have the strength to repent. Today, many people do not know any more how to ask forgiveness. They nail again the Son of God to the Cross. So, I wanted to come and recall it to you, especially here in Rwanda, for here I have still found humble people, who are not attached to wealth nor money."* Our Lady asked us to recite this chaplet every day if we can, but especially Fridays, September 14, the feast of the Holy Cross; and on September 15, the feast of Our Lady of Seven Sorrows. She also stated that she did not just come for Rwanda, or Africa but when she comes to speak to us her words are for the entire world (iii).

Our Lord was many things to many people: presumed political leader, prophet, healer, messiah, Lord and God-Man. To His mother He was always one thing: her little boy, her heart, her purpose in life and gift from God. As one ponders the seven sorrows of this devotion it is important not only to emphasize with the suffering that any mother would have at the sight of her son beaten, bloody and slowly dying, but to realize that just as Our Lord sacrificed and suffered for us, so did his mother.

She was born without sin and never committed a mortal sin. Thus, both she and her Son were innocent victims of all the sin that will ever be. His passion was the giving of his life for the world and her task was to give her son back to God. One can imagine her quietly smiling to herself when others would speak of the wisdom that came from his lips and the miracles done by his hands in His public ministry. Quietly smiling and thinking, "That's my little boy, my son." Being free from sin, the greatest love the immaculate and sacred hearts could only result in the deepest heart break in the passion of the Lord. The immaculate heart of our mother and the Sacred Heart of Jesus would ache beyond our understanding to see the other in pain. How great the pain Our Lord had to bear and how deep the sorrow of the mother compelled by love to witness the passion and death of her only Son. Our Lord is pleased when we reflect on the sorrow and pain of his mother and our lady is moved when we meditate on the Passion of her Son.

The Catechism of the Church states: *"Mary's role in the Church is inseparable from her union with Christ and flows directly from it. This union of the mother with the Son in the work of salvation is made manifest from the time of Christ's virginal conception up to his death; it is made manifest above all at the hour of his Passion: Thus, the Blessed Virgin advanced in her pilgrimage of faith, and faithfully persevered in her union with her Son unto the cross. There she stood, in keeping with the divine plan, enduring with her only begotten Son the intensity of his suffering, joining herself with his sacrifice in her mother's heart, and lovingly consenting to the immolation of this victim, born of her: to be given, by the same Christ Jesus dying on the cross, as a mother to his disciple, with these words: 'Woman, behold your son (iv)."*

One does not have to look far to see reasons why Our Blessed Mother would still have reason to cry. Her son founded one church according to the Gospel and now there are approximately 33,000 Churches that claim to be Christian. In the Gospel of John, He plainly prays to Our Father that we be one as He and His Father are one and He clearly establishes one church when He says to Peter, "You are the rock upon which I build MY church," not churches.

We are, unfortunately, also a church in the crisis due to clerical sexual abuse. Lust and objectification of the human person are undermining the sanctity of marriage simultaneously. Man has taken the authority of God as arbitrator of life and death and placed that crown on his own head. New York is one state that recently approved laws that essentially sanction abortion on demand and the current Governor of Virginia, a medical doctor, supports the same agenda in his state. The nation of Ireland recently came to the same conclusion. Porn sites attract more visitors each month than Amazon, Netflix, and Twitter combined, and thirty percent of Internet content is porn (v). Many school aged children have cell phones that give them free internet access and, without supervision, access to a world of darkness.

Fifty-Eight percent of American Catholics favor abortion in most cases (vi). There are times when I hear the priest say, "look not on our sins, but the faith of your church..." and I cringe slightly. The gospels relate that in certain towns Jesus "did not perform many miracles due to their lack of faith (Mt 13:54 – 58)." If faith is a verb and something reflected by what we do, where is our faith? How can we expect "God to come to our assistance and make haste to help us" when, as a culture, we increasingly do not believe Him evident by falling numbers of those who say they are Christian? Many today see him merely as moral teacher on par with Buddha and not the Word made flesh. In a society that has baptized itself in relativism we assert there is a plurality of truths with equal merit despite the fact there was One among us who stated "I am the way and (THE) truth and the life. No one comes to the Father except through me, (Jn 14:6)."

As of April 5, 2018, California, Colorado and the District of Columbia, Oregon, Vermont, and Washington have "death with dignity statutes. The Hawaii statute, approved in 2018, went into effect on January 1, 2019. In Montana, physician-assisted dying has been legal by State Supreme Court ruling since 2009. Evil is what happens when good men and women sit idly by and do nothing. Nazi Germany began the practice of genocide by first legalizing abortion and the euthanasia of those seen to be a burden of society-the developmentally disabled and deformed. As Catholics we have the privilege of being God's church and the people, he repeatedly sends his mother to plead with us to repent and live the faith that we profess to amend what is escalating in the world. Our Blessed Mother plead with us at both Fatima Portugal and Kibeho Rwanda.

Pope Leo XIII had a vision of the 20th century that indicated it was a time the devil would be allowed more power than before. In response he wrote the prayer to St. Michael and taught that it would be said at the conclusion of every mass. The 20th century has now passed and, while there were astronomical leaps and bounds in technology and science compared to other ages, there were two world wars, multiple efforts to "ethnically cleanse" entire populations, the rise and fall of communism and host of other examples of the demonic unveiling itself. No one wants the answer to the question," ...when the Son of Man comes, will he find faith on earth? (Lk 18:8)"to be, "No." One would hope that the Lord would not allow the eclipse of good in the world to be entire.

At the same time there were examples of people pulling together to make a better world in the civil rights movement, putting a man on the moon, vaccines for polio and other illnesses that previously crippled or killed amongst other great accomplishments. It is up to us, as the people of God in the church He founded, to take up the spiritual arms at our disposal

40

and participate in the divine plan to save the world. There is a saying in the Talmud, "If one saves another person, they save the world." Of all creation only the human mind can contemplate the universe. Our Lord endured His passion with a love that, if only one soul existed in all time, He still would have suffered the cross for that one soul.

We are who he calls. He shed His blood for us when we were still his enemies. Prayer changes the universe and human history whether readily perceived, or not. Having free will we can be presented with the truth and the way to live it and still say, "No thank you." Who on earth would really want to be that person?

Opening Prayers

Of the Sorrowful Rosary of Our Lady:

I offer you this rosary Lord for your greater glory, my own conversion and that of the world through your Son, my God and savior, Jesus Christ. May I please increase in my love of you and my fellows as I accompany my holy mother in the sorrows of her earthly life; grow in my appreciation of the price paid for my salvation in precious blood; and come to prefer death over ever seriously offending You again. As I attempt to console our Blessed Mother, may I appreciate more how much You and she did, and do, and have suffered due to sin and how much rejoicing there is in heaven at the conversion of a single soul. Amen.

Lord, I am sorry for my sins. In choosing to do what is wrong and failing to do what is good, I not only dread the loss of heaven and the reality of hell, but I offend you who I can only rightly love above all else. I do hope that, with the continued help of your grace and strength to confess and do penance for my sin, continue to amend my life and avoid sin and the occasion of it. Lord Jesus Christ Son of a living God have mercy on me a sinner. Amen.

How to Pray Rosary of Our Lady of Sorrows

3x Hail Mary for the tears shed by our blessed mother.

O, Lord come to my assistance.

O, God make haste to help me.

Glory be to the Father, Son and Holy Spirit as it was in the beginning is now and ever shall be a world without end. Amen.

The prophecy of Simeon:

"...Simeon blessed them and said to Mary his mother, "Behold, this child is destined for the fall and rise of many in Israel, and to be a sign that will be contradicted (and you yourself a sword will pierce) so that the thoughts of many hearts may be revealed (Lk 2:34-35)."

Sorrowful mother, I imagine you going to the Temple in joy to present your son with St. Joseph. Once there, you encounter Simeon who predicts that not only will your infant child be rejected, you too will suffer in the course of doing God's will. How shocked you must have been to hear this proclamation. Contrasted with the news of Gabriel that your son would ascend to the throne of his father David, pondering the predictions of Simeon must have tugged at your heart and concerned you greatly. Pray for me sorrowful mother that when God's will breaks my heart, I will have faith He will also make it whole again. *1x Our Father & 7x Hail Mary.*

Mary, conceived without sin who suffered for us, pray for us and give us a deeper appreciation of your Son and His sacrifice.

The flight to Egypt:

...the angel of the Lord appeared to Joseph in a dream and said, "Rise, take the child and his mother, flee to Egypt, and stay there until I tell you. Herod is going to search for the child to destroy him." Joseph rose and took the child and his mother by night and departed for Egypt. He stayed there until the death of Herod, that what the Lord had said through the prophet might be fulfilled, "Out of Egypt I called my son, (Mt 2:13-15)."

Sorrowful mother, I imagine how much you must have feared for your new, small family as you fled into the unknown due to St. Joseph's dream. How difficult it must have been, after being the subject of judgement, gossip and ignorant criticisms having been found pregnant out of wedlock, you and your small family were uprooted from all things familiar in order to protect your infant child from the diabolical wrath of Herod. A child so small and yet being the One who framed the universe. Pray for me sorrowful mother, that I may always place God and his kingdom first above all else. *1x Our Father& 7x Hail Mary.*

Mary, conceived without sin who suffered for us, pray for us and give us a deeper appreciation of your Son and his sacrifice.

The finding of the child Jesus at the Temple:

"After three days they found him in the temple, sitting in the midst of the teachers, listening to them and asking them questions, and all who heard him were astounded at his understanding and his answers. When his parents saw him, they were astonished, and his mother said to him, "Son, why have you done this to us? Your father and I have been looking for you with great anxiety, (Lk 2:46-48)."

Sorrowful mother, I imagine your heart dropping in your chest at the realization that your son could not be found in the caravan. How frantic and desperate you and St. Joseph must have been not to find him. Possibly fears that he was hurt, or evil befallen him fueled the panic that possibly he was lost forever. What relief and consternation you must have had to find him well and in eager discourse with elders at the holy Temple. Pray for me sorrowful mother, that when all seems lost, I will have the faith that your Devine Son is right where he is supposed to be, and I am the one that needs to find Him. *1x Our Father & 7x Hail Mary.*

Mary, conceived without sin, who suffered for us, pray for us and give us a deeper appreciation of your Son and his sacrifice.

Our blessed mother meets Jesus on the way to Calvary:

"A large crowd of people followed Jesus, including many women who mourned and lamented him (LK 23:27)."

Sorrowful mother, I find it difficult to imagine or comprehend your seeing your precious son so badly beaten, bloody, stumbling and falling under the weight of the cross. When he was a child you could pick him up, dust him off and give him a kiss to ease his pain. Now as you see the child you raised to manhood wounded and subject to the jeers of the crowd, I can only imagine how helpless and powerless you felt. In your heart I believe you would be willing to suffer in your Son's place just as he was enduring his suffering for me and all humanity. Other women present, total strangers were bereft at the sight of what had been done to your son. Pray for me sorrowful mother, that though I, too, will fall, I can rise again with grace from your son and under your loving eye. *1x Our Father & 7x Hail Mary.*

Mary, conceived without sin who suffered for us, pray for us and give us a deeper appreciation of your Son and his sacrifice.

Jesus suffers and dies on the cross:

"Standing by the cross of Jesus were his mother and his mother's sister, Mary the wife of Clopas, and Mary of Magdala. When Jesus saw his mother and the disciple there whom he loved, he said to his mother, 'Woman, behold, your son.' Then he said to the disciple, 'Behold, your mother.' And from that hour the disciple took her into his home. After this, aware that everything was now finished, in order that the scripture might be fulfilled, Jesus said, 'I thirst'...When Jesus had taken the wine, he said, 'It is finished.' And bowing his head, he handed over the spirit (Jn 19:25-28, 30)."

Sorrowful mother, I cannot imagine the powerlessness, grief and despair you must have felt at the foot of the cross watching your son slowly die over six hours of agony. Because of your love for your son, you were willing to witness what no mother should have to see. The pain must have cut to your very soul as you saw your only son beaten and pierced upon the cross. How you must have winced as the nails were driven into his hands and feet. The horror and trauma of the moment must have led you to be oblivious to your surroundings as you were focused on your son and the aching, weight in your heart. Sorrowful mother pray for me that every day that I am grateful for the gift of my life-a life given to me by your Son since he gave His life for mine. *1x Our Father & 7x Hail Mary.*

Mary, conceived without sin, who suffered for us, pray for us and give us a deeper appreciation of your Son and his sacrifice.

Jesus is taken down from the cross:

"Nicodemus, the one who had first come to him at night, came bringing a mixture of myrrh and aloes weighing about one hundred pounds. They took the body of Jesus and bound it with burial cloths along with the spices, according to the Jewish burial custom, (Jn 19:39-40)."

Sorrowful mother, the tears of joy shed while holding your son at his birth have turned to rivers of deepest sorrow. No mother expects to hold the lifeless body of their own child. How it must have torn you to the core just moments before as the solider thrust his lance into the already destroyed body of your child. Holding that body now, I imagine your feelings could only be expressed by wordless sobbing. *1x Our Father & 7x Hail Mary.*

Mary conceived without sin, who suffered for us, pray for us and give us a deeper appreciation of your Son and his sacrifice.

Jesus is laid in the tomb:

"It was the day of preparation, and the sabbath was about to begin. The women who had come from Galilee with him followed behind, and when they had seen the tomb and the way in which his body was laid in it (Lk 23:54-55)."

Sorrowful mother I imagine you must have been despondent as the stone to your precious son's tomb was rolled into place. The finality of the silence after that moment was the final twist in the sword that pierced your heart. The shock and trauma of the day and watching your son slowly die for six hours had to have taken its toll on you. I Imagine sadness clinging to you like a shawl draped over you fallen shoulders and covering your down turned head. I can see you slowly walking away from the tomb with St. John and in silence with blank expressions on every face. Your eyes now dry and read from having exhausted all the tears of your poor maternal heart. *1x Our Father &7x Hail Mary.*

Mary, conceived without sin, who suffered for us, pray for us and give us a deeper appreciation of your Son and his sacrifice.

Closing Prayer

I thank you Lord that I am now better acquainted with you, your mother and the personal cost paid to give me life. I will never be able to fully appreciate how much you both have done for me while I am on earth. I do praise, glorify and bless the Eternal Father for sending your Son, Lord Jesus; I praise, glorify and bless you for by your holy life, passion, cross and resurrection you have conquered the world, sin and death to set me free; I praise glorify and bless your holy mother and St. Joseph for saying "Yes..." to God's will. I am Grateful for the Living, Holy Spirit which you have sent to guide us and to renew the face of the earth. Amen.

The Little Crown of the Blessed Virgin Mary

According to St. Louis Marie de Montfort:

Then God's temple in heaven was opened, and the ark of his covenant could be seen in the temple. There were flashes of lightning, rumblings, and peals of thunder, an earthquake, and a violent hailstorm. A great sign appeared in the sky, a woman clothed with the sun, with the moon under her feet, and on her head a crown of twelve stars (Rev 11:19-12:1).

Introductory Prayer
Come, Holy Spirit, fill the hearts of Thy faithful and kindle within them the fire of Thy love!

V. Send forth Thy Spirit and they shall be created.
R. And Thou shalt renew the face of the earth.

Let us pray.
O God, who by the light of the Holy Spirit dost instruct the hearts of the faithful, grant us by this same Spirit to relish what is right and ever to rejoice in His consolation, through Christ our Lord. Amen.

I-Crown of Excellence
To honor the divine maternity of the Blessed Virgin, her ineffable virginity, her purity without stain and her innumerable virtues.
V. Grant that I may praise thee, Holy Virgin!
R. Give me strength against thy enemies!

Our Father.
Hail Mary.
Blessed art thou, O Virgin Mary, who didst hear the Lord, the Creator of the world; thou didst give birth to Him Who made thee and remainest a Virgin forever.
Rejoice, O Virgin Mary! Rejoice a thousand times!
2.) Hail Mary.
O holy and immaculate Virgin, I know not with what praise to extol thee, since thou didst bear in thy womb the very one Whom the heavens cannot contain.
Rejoice, O Virgin Mary! Rejoice a thousand times!
3.) Hail Mary.
Thou art all fair, O Virgin Mary, and there is no stain in thee.
Rejoice, O Virgin Mary! Rejoice a thousand times!

4.) Hail Mary.
Thy virtues, O Virgin, surpass the stars of heaven in number.
Rejoice, O Virgin Mary! Rejoice a thousand times!
Glory be.

II-Crown of Power
To honor the royalty of the Blessed Virgin, her magnificence, her universal mediation and the strength of her rule.

5.) Our Father.
Hail Mary.
Glory be to thee, O Empress of the world! Bring us with thee to the joy of Heaven.
Rejoice, O Virgin Mary! Rejoice a thousand times!
6.) Hail Mary.
Glory be to thee, O treasure house of the Lord's graces! Grant us a share in thy riches.
Rejoice, O Virgin Mary! Rejoice a thousand times!
7.) Hail Mary.
Glory be to thee, O Mediatrix between God and man! Through thee may the Almighty be favorable to us.
Rejoice, O Virgin Mary! Rejoice a thousand times!
8.) Hail Mary.
Glory be to thee who destroyest heresies and crushest demons! Be thou our loving guide.
Rejoice, O Virgin Mary! Rejoice a thousand times!
Glory be.

III-Crown of Goodness
To honor the mercy of the Blessed Virgin toward sinners, the poor, the just and the dying. 9.) Our Father.
Hail Mary.
Glory be to thee, O refuge of sinners! Intercede for us with God!
Rejoice, O Virgin Mary! Rejoice a thousand times!

10.) Hail Mary.

Glory be to thee, O Mother of Orphans! Render the Almighty favorable to us.

Rejoice, O Virgin Mary! Rejoice a thousand times!

11.) Hail Mary.

Glory be to thee O, joy of the just! Lead us with thee to the joys of Heaven.

Rejoice, O Virgin Mary! Rejoice a thousand times!

12.) Hail Mary.

Glory be to thee who art ever ready to assist us in life and in death! Lead us with thee to the kingdom of Heaven!

Rejoice, O Virgin Mary! Rejoice a thousand times!

Glory be.

Let us pray

Hail Mary, Daughter of God the Father; Hail Mary, Mother of God the Son; Hail Mary, Spouse of the Holy Spirit; Hail Mary, Temple of the Most Holy Trinity; Hail Mary, my mistress, my treasure, my joy, Queen of my heart; my Mother, my life, my sweetness, my dearest hope, yea, my heart and my soul! I am all thine, and all that I have is thine, O Virgin blessed above all things! Let thy soul be in me to magnify the Lord; let thy spirit be in me to rejoice in God. Set thyself, O faithful Virgin, as a seal upon my heart, that in thee and through thee I may be found faithful to God. Receive me, O gracious Virgin, among those whom thou loves and teaches, whom thou leads, nourish and protect as thy children. Grant that for love of thee I may despise all earthly consolations and ever cling to those of Heaven; until through the Holy Ghost, thy faithful Spouse, and through thee, His faithful Spouse, Jesus Christ thy Son be formed in me for the glory of the Father. Amen.

OUR LORD'S PROMISES ATTACHED TO THE PRAYING OF THE CHAPLET OF

DIVINE MERCY AS REVEALED TO ST. FAUSTINA KOWALSKA
FROM HER DIARY (vii)

"I promise that the soul that will venerate this image (of Divine Mercy) will not perish. I also promise victory over (its) enemies already here on earth, especially at the hour of death. I Myself will defend it as My own glory (*Diary*, **48**)."

"The souls that say this chaplet will be embraced by My mercy during their lifetime and especially at the hour of their death (*Diary*, **754**)."

"When hardened sinners say it, I will fill their souls with peace, and the hour of their death will be a happy one (*Diary*, **1541**)."

"When they say this chaplet in the presence of the dying, I will stand between My Father and the dying person, not as a just Judge but as a merciful Savior (*Diary*, **1541**)."

"Whoever will recite it will receive great mercy at the hour of death (*Diary*, **687**)."

"Priests will recommend it to sinners as their last hope of salvation. Even if there were a sinner most hardened, if he were to recite this chaplet only once, he would receive grace from My infinite mercy...I desire to grant unimaginable graces to those souls who trust in My mercy (*Diary*, **687**)."

"To priests who proclaim and extol My mercy, I will give wondrous power; I will anoint their words and touch the hearts of those to whom they will speak (*Diary*, **1521**)."

"The prayer most pleasing to Me is prayer for the conversion for sinners. Know, my daughter, that this prayer is always heard and answered (*Diary*, **1397**)."

"At three o'clock, implore My mercy, especially for sinners; and, if only for a brief moment, immerse yourself in My Passion, particularly in My abandonment at the moment of agony...I will refuse nothing to the soul that makes a request of Me in virtue of My Passion (*Diary*, **1320; Also cf.** *Diary*, **1572**)."

"Souls who spread the honor of My mercy...at the hour of death I will not be a Judge for them, but the Merciful Savior (*Diary*, **1075**)."

"The two rays denote Blood and Water...These two rays issued from the very depths of My tender mercy when My agonized Heart was opened by a lance on the Cross. These rays shield souls from the wrath of My Father...I desire that the first Sunday after Easter be the Feast of Mercy...whoever approaches the Fount of Life on this day will be granted complete remission of sins and punishment. Mankind will not have peace until it turns with trust to My mercy (*Diary*, **299-300**)."

"I desire that the Feast of Mercy...be solemnly celebrated on the first Sunday after Easter...The soul that will go to Confession and receive Holy Communion (in a state of grace on this day) shall obtain complete forgiveness of sins and punishment (*Diary*, **699**)."

"Through this chaplet you will obtain everything, if what you ask for is compatible with My will (*Diary*, **1731**)."

"My mercy is greater than your sins and those of the entire world (*Diary*, **1485**)."

Prayers of the Chaplet of Mercy

These are said on ordinary rosary beads

Make the sign of the cross and kiss the crucifix.

Optional opening prayer; You expired, Jesus, but the source of life gushed forth for souls, and the ocean of mercy opened for the whole world. O Fount of Life, unfathomable Divine Mercy, envelop the whole world and empty Yourself out upon us.

Second optional opening prayer: O Blood and Water which gushed forth from the heart of Jesus as a fount of mercy for us, I trust in you. Said 3x.

1. Say the Our Father x1.
2. Say the Hail Mary x1.
3. The Apostles Creed: I believe in God, the Father almighty, Creator of heaven and earth, and in Jesus Christ, His only Son, our Lord, who was conceived by the Holy Spirit, born of the Virgin Mary, suffered under Pontius Pilate, was crucified, died and was buried; He descended into hell; on the third day He rose again from the dead; He ascended into heaven, and is seated at the right hand of God the Father almighty; from there He will come to judge the living and the dead. I believe in the Holy Spirit, the holy catholic Church, the communion of saints, the forgiveness of sins, the resurrection of the body, and life everlasting. Amen.

4. On the large beads at the beginning of each decade: O Eternal Father, I offer you the body, blood, soul and divinity of your dearly beloved son, Our Lord Jesus Christ, in atonement for our sins and those of the whole world.

5. On the ten beads of the decade: For the sake of his sorrowful passion, have mercy on us and on the whole world.

Repeat the O Eternal Father and for the sake of his sorrowful passion prayers on each decade as noted above.

6. At the conclusion say 3x: Holy God, Holy Mighty One, Holy Eternal One-have mercy on us and on the whole world.

Optional closing prayer: Eternal God, in whom mercy is endless and the treasury of compassion — inexhaustible, look kindly upon us and increase Your mercy in us, so that in difficult moments, we might not despair nor become despondent but, with great confidence submit ourselves to Your holy will, which is Love and Mercy itself.

Ways to Meditate with the Chaplet of Mercy

People tend to wonder how to meditate when reciting the Chaplet of Devine Mercy. One thought is to focus on one wound acquired by Our Lord in his passion or the five stigmata for each decade; 1-the crown of thorns, 2-the nail in his right wrist, 3-the nail in his left wrist, 4-the nail in his feet, 5-the piercing of his side. Or one can use this guide taken from the Diary of St. Sister Faustina to whom the chaplet was revealed:

Meditation upon His wounds pleases Jesus and benefits us and all humanity as well. That can motivate us to reflect upon them. Further, His mercy is manifested in these wounds, since He sacrificed Himself for our sins and for those sins committed against us. "Jesus told me that I please Him best by meditating on His sorrowful Passion and by such meditation much light falls upon my soul. He who wants to learn true humility should reflect upon the Passion of Jesus. I get a clear under-standing of many things that I could not comprehend before" (Diary, 267). Jesus also suggested, "When it seems to you that your suffering exceeds your strength, contemplate My wounds..." (Diary, 1184, 1512).

The Chaplet of Divine Mercy can help us dwell on the wounds of our Lord while we use the five decades of our rosary beads. When trying to pray the chaplet, many find some difficulty with concentration. It is inevitable that we become unfocused in our prayer life. Having distractions during the recitation of the chaplet will be no exception. However, when we meditate on the meaning of these sacred wounds, we deepen our appreciation of what Our Lord had to endure, and our prayer life can be greatly enriched (See Diary, 737). It is easier to stay focused on our Lord's passion, or anything else when meditating, the more one engages their imagination. When one attempts to see the scene through the eyes of a bystander, or how our Lord looked after being so cruelly beaten, etc.

There is no best way to focus on Christ's wounds. The following suggestions are offered, not only to help control the many intrusive thoughts we may experience in prayer, but more importantly, to gently deepen our understanding of what is conveyed by each individual wound. When we focus on the symbolism of these wounds, we say the chaplet with greater fervor. Each wound may have a personal meaning for us. Continued reflection on what Jesus endured can enable us to be convicted by the message that Our Lord is trying to communicate. We permit ourselves a greater familiarity with His suffering in order to continue honoring His great personal sacrifice for us. Thus, an otherwise routine experience has been transformed into an uplifting time of prayer.

The First Decade: Since the crown of thorns is so apparent, we can begin our meditation on this part of His sacrifice. We dwell on the multiple wounds caused by the thorns. These were real, not just symbolic. Our attention is drawn to the awareness that Jesus did not save us by His teaching alone. We see how He bore the insults heaped upon him by the Roman soldiers. He was forced to wear the humiliating crown of thorns that mocked His kingship and authority over us. We can recognize in the soldiers' mockery of Jesus our willfulness and wanting to be our own authority. While contemplating the sacred wounds to Our Lord's head, we remain in awe that He accepted the punishment due to our sinful "thought life." His acceptance of each thorn gives us a compelling realization that there are consequences of sins committed in our minds and that all others have their origin in a thought. In the Gospel of Matthew 15:19, we read: "From the mind stem evil designs - murder, adulterous conduct, fornication, stealing, false witness, blasphemy." All sins first begin in our minds. Our Lord had to make atonement to the Father not only for the sins of the mind, but for our yielding to these sins. Each thorn represents another opportunity for us to be grateful to Jesus for having endured all this for us and what he has spared us. In her diary, St. Sister Faustina describes the vision of hell she was given at section 741.

By the same token, He suffered the anguish for the sins of those who falsely accuse us of transgressions. These negative judgments must be expiated. Our Lord also loves the very ones who make these accusations and takes upon Himself the sorrow and grief that these sins have caused. Jesus revealed the degree of His mercy by enduring the reparation for the sins of injustice. Through this action, He not only atoned but extended forgiveness as well, with the expectation that we would find room in our mind and heart to likewise convey mercy and compassion. What if we are not forgiving? What are the consequences of resentment, of our rage and desire for vengeance? Many individuals, weighed down with bitterness and unforgiveness, are drained of life-giving energy. Eventually, this attitude can block out the experience of being forgiven.

Many are burdened with toxic guilt and have no recourse to alleviate their consciences. Only God can atone for these as well. For them, too, Jesus had to endure the crown of thorns. In her diary, Our Lord is quoted as saying "Tell souls not to place within their own hearts obstacles to My mercy, which greatly wants to act in them. My mercy works in all those hearts that which open their doors to it. Both the sinner and the righteous per son have need of My mercy. Conversion, as well as perseverance is a grace of My mercy (Diary, 1577)."

The Second Decade: During the second decade, we reflect on the wound that pierced His right wrist. We are moved to venerate and acknowledge His pain by seeing ourselves embrace that wound. In faith, we accept the notion that, out of His love for us, Jesus made reparation for the sins committed by the right hand and those that are committed with full knowledge and intent. Examples of this include some who have acted out toward others in rage, stolen things, touched some-one inappropriately, or violated another. Jesus had to suffer as a result of these actions. In justice, He was willing to suffer due to these sins.

Similarly, Our Lord experienced great sorrow on account of those who, for whatever reason, struck out against us. He was willing to suffer for those who abused us as a result of their anger. For many, these memories and events are not easily relinquished or forgiven. Countless individuals carry these memories for years and others for a lifetime. Multitudes die, unwilling to forgive those who offended them. Our Lord atoned for these actions and for the lack of forgiveness as well.

The Third Decade: We follow the same pattern but reflect on the wound in Jesus' left hand or wrist. We again venerate, honor, and embrace this wound which He was willing to accept in atonement to His Father for the violations committed with this hand. This action of Jesus represents His willingness to take upon Himself all the punishment due to our complicity and cavalier attitude toward sin. Our Lord's sacrifice reveals that there is no trivializing the way He endured the physical anguish caused by a callous attitude toward sin. It was painfully real. The nails did penetrate His hands and feet, blood did flow, and His agony continued unabated. After the Resurrection, He even made all the apostles aware of the wounds in His hands and side and invited Thomas to probe them for himself. (see Jn. 20:27). That same invitation is ours to accept and come to appreciate every time we pray the chaplet.

The left hand is often considered to be of minor importance in various cultures. For our purpose, it serves as a metaphor for being insensitive to the needs of others who need to forgive us. Our indifference to the beggar or the plight of another person who needs our assist also needs atonement. Our sins of omission or insensitive mistreatment of others cry out to heaven for justice. Jesus accepted the grief of those left behind through cultural differences, lack of proper upbringing, the intolerance of certain religions, and a lack of compassion toward the poor and marginalized. We also acknowledge that our Lord endured the suffering due to the sins against those who were abandoned, either in the womb or through someone's unwillingness to care for them.

The Fourth Decade: On the fourth decade, we pause to venerate the wounds in Our Lord's feet. We inwardly adore Jesus by becoming ever more grateful that He accepted the penetrating nails in atonement for the sins of the whole world.

We sense that He is conveying to us His purpose for accepting this violent action against His Person.

He took upon Himself the punishment of those whose sin consisted in walking away from the Church, the Sacraments, and the teachings of the faith. Many walk away from the influence of the word of God, which was intended to teach us the right path upon which to walk. Others have had a negative influence on their families through many generations and have caused others to depart from the faith. The accumulation of all these influences results in many losing their souls for all eternity. Others have willfully walked away due to pride and subjective determinations about their own lives. Many have walked away from their marriage vows and their commitment to their families, especially their children. There is confusion caused by priests and religious who pronounced vows and then abandon their commitments. If the dwindling numbers of priests and religious indicate anything, it may be that many are having the call to religious life and the priesthood drowned out by the noise of cultural trends and the world. Due to these gross violations against the overwhelming love of God the Father, Jesus necessarily atoned for them all. When we unite ourselves to Our Lord in praying for these souls, we pray with great confidence since Our Lord said: "The prayer most pleasing to Me is prayer for the conversion of sinners (Diary, 1397)."

The Fifth Decade: Centuries after our Merciful Savior accomplished His incomparable sacrifice on the cross, He seeks to deepen our understanding of what He personally suffered for us. He asks us, through St. Faustina, to pray the chaplet as an atonement for our sins and the sins of the whole world. Our Lord told her "While there is still time, let them have recourse to My mercy; Let them profit from the water and blood that gushed forth for them (Diary, 848)." Our Lord revealed to Saint Faustina, through the painting of the Divine Mercy image, just how much it meant for Him to shed the last of His Blood and Water, which flowed from His open side. We again adore, venerate, and honor this awesome reminder of the unyielding compassion with which Jesus was willing to sacrifice Himself for us. He did this not only in words, but in the fullness of being. He endured the shame of the cross and was abandoned by those to whom He gave so much of Himself.

Some people experience abandonment from divorce and must live with the unresolved consequences even though they may have asked repeatedly for a blessed marriage. Some suffer the loss of a spouse through death, and that loss may seem intolerable. Some endure a terminal illness, even though many prayers and sacrifices were offered for healing. Some live alone or in an institution. Some are imprisoned, physically or in their mind. Some have maintained their integrity in every respect but have failed in their attempts to overcome a problem or achieve a specific goal and purpose in life. When he declared: "Father, why have You forsaken Me (Mk 15:34)?" He is expressing a similar type of hopelessness. "Do not despair. I know what you are experiencing. Look to Me. See how I yielded Myself to the Father and conquered sin and the grave. We too can pray with abandon, `Into Your hands I submit my spirit (Lk 23:46).'" These last words of Jesus can bring power, healing, and resolution to seemingly hopeless situations. The secret to our healing and union with Jesus is in surrendering as He did. To the degree we yield to God, to that degree we are in union with Him. St. Sister Faustina stated joining one's will to God is what truly makes one free (Diary, 462).

In focusing upon the five wounds of Lord and what He singularly accomplished for us, we come to the inevitable conclusion that, in faith, we can choose to trust Him because of all He has done to merit our confidence. We join our prayers with a multitude of others and profess: Blood and Water which gushed forth from the Heart of Jesus, as a fount of mercy for us, I trust in You!

True Devotion to the Blessed Virgin Mary Total Consecration to Jesus Through Mary:

St Louis Marie de Montfort is the apostle of Mary. His books *The Secret of the Rosary, The Secret of Mary* and *True Devotion to Mary* leave no doubt that Our Lord's words from the cross, "Behold you mother..." were spoken to all of us. How and why our blessed mother not only served as the mother of our Lord but continues to serve God as the surest way for us to reach Him.

The essence of true devotion to our Blessed Mother as an act of surrender of oneself to her entirely--including all that one has and can offer including material goods--to be used by her for the coming of our Lord's kingdom. This also includes imitation of her and the virtues she possessed as the one that was conceived without sin. Nothing is withheld from Our Lady and all is to be rendered to Our Lord through her. To and for her and thereby to and for Him to be used at her discretion as Queen of Heaven. While we are told to pray for others and their needs, even our intentions and all our sacrifices are the property of Mary. One allows her to use as she disposes, not necessarily for our own good, but for the greatest good possible and ultimate glory of God. Amongst God's creatures only Mary has the comprehension and far-reaching vision possible to take what we offer, refine it and turn it over to Our High Priest, her Son. By forming our heart to hers, she forms our hearts to His.

There is a 33-day preparation for this act of consecration which is a prayer by St. Louis de Montfort that readies one to make the offering of oneself to Jesus through Mary. The preparation involves daily meditations to be read and prayers to be said that focus on four themes: 1.) The renunciation of the spirit of the world: "Examine your conscience, pray, practice renouncement of your own will, mortification and purity of heart..." the things that arise in us that are of the world and barriers to spiritual health. 2.) Knowledge of self: "Prayers, examens, reflections, acts of renouncement of our own will, of contrition for our sins, of contempt of self, all at the feet of Mary for it is from her that we hope for the light to know ourselves.." 3.) Knowledge of Mary: "Acts of love, pious affections for the blessed virgin, imitation of her virtues, especially her profound humility, her lively faith, her blind obedience, her continual mental prayer, her mortifications in all things, her surpassing charity, her heroic patience, her angelic sweetness and her divine wisdom these being her ten principal virtues..." 4.) Knowledge of the Lord Jesus Christ: "First, the Man-God, His grace and glory; than His rights to sovereign dominion over us..." since we reject satan and claim Him as Lord. "Second: His interior life, namely, the virtues and acts of His Sacred Heart and His association with Mary (viii).

Adoration of Our Lord:

The heart of our Catholic faith is the consecration of the body and blood of our Lord at Mass and our reception Him that He may live in us. Adoration is contemplation and prayer in the presence of the consecrated host-the body, blood, soul, and divinity of Our Lord. This is not a substitute for the mass nor receiving our lord at holy communion. It is by virtue of the liturgy that the host is consecrated whether He is received at mass or adored in a monstrance or tabernacle. "The Catechism quotes St. John Paul II: 'The Church and the world have a great need for Eucharistic worship. Jesus awaits us in the sacrament of love. Let us not refuse the time to go to meet Him in adoration, in contemplation full of faith, and open to making amends for the serious offenses and crimes of the world (and our own sins). Let our adoration never cease(ix).

St. Teresa of Calcutta stated: "Perpetual Eucharistic Adoration with exposition needs a great push. People ask me, "What will convert America and save the world?' My answer is prayer. What we need is for every parish to come before Jesus in the Blessed Sacrament in holy hours of prayer (xi)." She also said: "The time you spend with Jesus in the Blessed Sacrament is the best time that you will spend on earth. Each moment that you spend with Jesus will deepen your union with Him and make your soul everlastingly more glorious and beautiful in heaven and will help bring about an everlasting peace on earth." She added: "Perpetual Adoration, Eucharistic Adoration offers to our people the opportunity to join those in religious life to pray for the salvation of the world, souls everywhere and peace on earth. We cannot underestimate the power of prayer and the difference it will make in our world (x)."

St. John Paul II taught that: " The Eucharist is a priceless treasure: by not only celebrating it, but also praying before it outside of Mass, we are enabled to contact the very wellspring of grace (xi). "The best, the surest and the most effective way of establishing peace on the face of the earth is through the great power of Perpetual Adoration of the Blessed Sacrament (xii)."

The Lord said, "I am with you always until the end of the age (Mt 28:20)." This is a profound truth of the love of God and it is nowhere more profound then when one is receiving or adoring the Eucharist. The practice of any devotion or prayer can only be enhanced by the fact that we are literally at the feet of Our Lord. Mary was seated at his feet while her sister Martha ran about franticly seeking to meet the needs of others. Our lord told her, "There is need of only one thing. Mary has chosen the better part and it will not be taken from her (Lk 10:42)." It is not possible for a Christian to say that time spent with our Lord would be better spent elsewhere. Most would agree that both St Teresa of Calcutta and St. John Paul II were very busy people on earth. Nonetheless, they started each day with at least one hour in adoration of Our Lord in the Blessed Sacrament. St. Frances de Sales said that everyone needs to spend at least 30 minutes a day in prayer, those that are busy, at least one hour a day. To know that prayer can suspend the laws of nature and end wars is not enough if no one is praying. It is hard to imagine what the world would be like if people gave up one hour of watching TV, videos or sports a week to simply be in the presence of the Lord, to worship, adore him and let him love you. That is who He is, why He came and as He remains with us in the Eucharist. All of which was proved and paid for by His precious blood. Simply try sitting with Our Lord for an hour. Staying awake with him for an hour was, in fact, the only thing recorded in the New Testament that He asked anyone to do for Him.

The following prayer is in gratitude by the author for countless blessings received in life.

Prayer of thanksgiving to Our Lord and Jesus to be said daily:

Most Sweet Lord Jesus Christ, in union with the unutterable praises which the Holy Trinity extolls upon Itself, Which thence flow from Your sacred humanity, upon Your holy mother, and all the angels and saints, I praise glorify and bless You for Yourself. Also, for the graces and privileges You have bestowed upon Your good friend and chosen apostle St. Jude. Through his intercession please come to my aid in all my needs and for the sake of his merits please strengthen and protect me against the rages and designs of all my enemies on this day you have made that we may rejoice and be glad, all the days of my life and on the final day, hours, and moments of my life. Amen. 3x Our Father, Hail Mary and Glory be.

References:

Catholic Church: *Catechism of the Catholic Church.* (2012) 2nd ed. Vatican: Libreria Editrice Vaticana, Rome Italy.

Kowalska, St. Maria Faustina. (2006). *Devine Mercy in my Soul; Dairy of St. Maria Faustina Kowalska.* Marian Press, Stockbridge MA.

Montfort Publications. (2005). *Preparation for Total Consecration According to St. Luis Marie de Montfort.* Montfort Publications, Bay Shore NY.

St John Paul II. (1998, May 31). *Dies Domini: To Bishops, Clergy and Faithful of the Catholic Church on Keeping Sunday Holy.* Retrieved on 2/20/2016 from https://w2.vatican.va/content/john-paul.../hf_jp-ii_apl_05071998_dies-domini.html.

St John Paul II. (1986, May 18). *Dominum Et Vivificantem: On the Holy Spirit in the Life of the Church and the World.* Retrieved on 5/22/2016 from: https://w2.vatican.va/content/john-paul-ii/en/encyclicals/documents/hf_jp-ii_enc_18051986_dominum-et-vivificantem.html#-35.

St John Paul II. (1995, March 25). *Evangelium Vitae.* Retrieved on 1/25/2016 from: http://w2.vatican.va/content/john-paul-ii/en/encyclicals/documents/hf_jpi_enc_25031995_evangelium-vitae.html. St

John Paul II. (1995, March 25). *General Audience: The Solemnity of the Annunciation of the Lord, in the year 1995.* Retrieved on 1/5/2017 from: http://www.catholicnewsagency.com/document/o-mary-bright-dawn-of-the-new-world-759/.

St John Paul II (Ed. Durepos, J. 2003). *Go in Peace: A Gift of Enduring Love*. Loyola Press, Chicago.

St John Paul II. (1982, May 20). *Homily for the Feast of the Ascension*. Retrieved on 6/22/2016 from: https://w2.vatican.va/content/john-paul-ii/it/homilies/1982/documents/hf_jp-ii_hom_19820520_ascensione.html St John Paul II. (2002, October 16). *Rosarium Virgins Mariae of the Supreme Pontiff St John Paul II to the Bishops. Clergy and Faithful of the Most Holy Rosary*. Retrieved on 1/23/2016 from http://www.ewtn.com/library/papaldoc/jp2rosar.htm.

St John Paul II. (1993, June 8). *Veritatis Splendor.* Retrieved on 5/29/2016 from: http://w2.vatican.va/content/john-paul-ii/en/encyclicals/documents/hf_jp-ii_enc_06081993_veritatls-splendor.html.

Endnotes:

i-United Conference of Catholic Bishops. (2019). *Prayer to St. Joseph After the Rosary.* Retrieved on 9/6/2019 from: http://www.usccb.org/prayer-and-worship/prayers-and-devotions/prayers/prayer-to-st-joseph-after-rosary.cfm.

ii-Our Catholic Prayers. (2018). *Promises of the Rosary of Our Lady of Sorrows.* Retrieved on 2/24/19 from: from https://www.ourcatholicprayers.com/Sorrowful-mothers-devotion-promises.html.

iii-Tardif, Therese. (10/1/2001). *Messages of Our Lady of Sorrows in Kibeho, Rwanda.* Retrieved on 1/254/19 from: https://www.michaeljournal.org/articles/roman-catholic-church/item/messages-of-our-lady-of-sorrows-in-kibeho-rwanda.

iv-*Catechism of the Catholic Church.* 2nd ed. Vatican: Librereia Editrice Vaticana. (2012). Print. Article 9, Paragraph 6:964.

v-Castleman, M. (11/6/2016). *Dueling Statistics: How Much of the Internet is Porn? In Psychology Today.* Retrieved on 2/24/19 from:https://www.psychologytoday.com/us/blog/all-about-sex/201611/dueling-statistics-how-much-the-internet-is-porn.

vi-Hartig, H. (10/17/18). *Nearly 6 in 10 Americans Say Abortion Should be Legal in Most Cases,* Retrieved on 2/24/19 from the Pew Research Journal website:

https://www.pewresearch.org/fact-tank/2018/10/17/nearly-six-in-ten-americans-say-abortion-should-be-legal/.

vii-Mendes, W. (1987). *Promises Attached to the Chaplet of Devine Mercy, Excerpts Taken from the Diary of St. Faustina Kowalska, Entitled Divine Mercy in My Soul.* Congregation of Marians of the Immaculate Conception, Stockbridge MA. Retrieved on 1/21/19 from: https://fathersofmercy.com/promises-attached-to-chaplet-of-divine-mercy/.

viii-Konokpa, L. (7/21/2009). *Contemplate My Wounds: Praying the Chaplet Opens Us to the Lessons of Christs Wounds.* Retrieved on 8/23/19 from: http://www.stmarysbeauly.org/uploads/9/5/8/8/9588114/contemplate_my_wounds.pdf.

ix-Montfort Publications. (2005). *Preparation for Total Consecration According to St. Louis Marie de Montfort.* Montfort Publications, Bayshore NY. pgs. 1, 21, 37 &56.

xi-United States Conference of Bishops. (2019). *Adoration.* Retrieved on 1/25/19 from: http://www.usccb.org/beliefs-and-teachings/vocations/adoration.cfm.

xii-St. Theresa of Calcutta. (2000). *Real Presence Eucharistic Association: The Real Presence, Christ in the Eucharist.* Retrieved on 1/25/19 from: http://www.therealpresence.org/eucharst/tes/quotes7.html.

xii- St. John Paul II. (4/17/2003). *Elcesia De Eucharistia.* Retrieved on 1/25/19 from the Vatican website at: http://www.vatican.va/holy_father/special_features/encyclicals/documents/hf_jp-ii_enc_20030417_ecclesia_eucharistia_en.html.

xiii- St. John Paul II. (6/13/1993). *Apostolic Journey to Spain: Speech of the Holy Father John Paul II to the National Delegates Participating in the XLV International Eucharistic Congress.* Retrieved and translated by the author from Spanish on the Vatican Website on 1/25/19 from; https://w2.vatican.va/content/john-paul-ii/es/speeches/1993/june/documents/hf_jp-ii_spe_19930613_delegati-congresso.html.

Printed in Great Britain
by Amazon

46071293R00040